Light Is Shining
in the Africa I Know

by

Henry Church

Light and Life Press
999 College Avenue
Winona Lake, Indiana 46590

Published for
Women's Missionary Fellowship International
Free Methodist Church

Cover and book design by John Benson
Edited by Mary C. Benson

Front cover photo by Henry Church

Printed in the United States of America
by Light and Life Press
Winona Lake, Indiana 46590

Copyright 1987 by
Light and Life Press

ISBN 0-89367-123-1

Africa

The people
that walked in darkness
have seen
a great light:
they that dwell
in the land
of the shadow of death,
upon them
hath the light shined.
— Isaiah 9:2

Pronunciation Guide
A Partial List

Vowels

a	ah	o	oh
e	ay	u	oo
i	ee	y	ee

Names of Places

Balaka	Bah lah' kah	Lilongwe	Lee lohng' way
Blantyre	Blahn tire	Luchenza	Loo chayn' zah
Chikombedzi	Chee kohm bed' zee	Lundi	Loon' dee
Chilenda	Chee layn' dah	Lusaka	Loo sah' kah
Chipata	Chee pah' tah	Malawi	Mah lah' wee
Chiredzi	Chee red' zee	Malawian	Mah lah' wee ahn
Chirundu	Chee roon' doo	Nkhatakota	Nkoh' tah koh' tah
Chitawa	Chee tah' wah	Salima	Sah lee' mah
Damba	Dahm' bah	Sanga	Sahn' gah
Gwengwe	Gwayne' gway	Zambezi	Zahm bay' zee
Harare	Hah rah' ray	Zimbabwe	Zeem bahb' way
Johannesburg	Joh hahn' ness burg	Zomba	Zohm' bah
Kurbula	Koor boo' lah		

Names of Persons, Languages, Money

Chauke Elesinah	Chah oo' kay Ay lay see' nah		
Chichewa	Chee chay' wah	Shangaan	Shahn' gahn
huma	hoo' mah	tambala	tahm bah' lah
kwatcha	kwah' chah		

Contents

AFRICA

SOUTHERN AFRICA

SCALE OF MILES
0   100   200   400   600

ZAIRE

ANGOLA

ZAMBIA

Lusaka

Lake Kariba

Zambezi River

MALAWI

Lake Malawi

NAMIBIA
(SOUTH-WEST
AFRICA)

Harare

ZIMBABWE

Lundi • Chiredzi

Lundi Bible School

Chikombedzi Hospital

BOTSWANA

MOZAMBIQUE

Beira

Limpopo River

Nhaloi
Massinga
Inhambane

TRANSVAAL

Inhamachafo

Pretoria

Johannesburg

Maputo
(Lourenço Marques)

REPUBLIC OF SOUTH AFRICA

ORANGE
FREE
STATE

NATAL

SWAZILAND

LESOTHO

Durban

Fairview

Greenville

ATLANTIC
OCEAN

CAPE OF
GOOD HOPE

TRANSKEI

INDIAN OCEAN

Cape Town

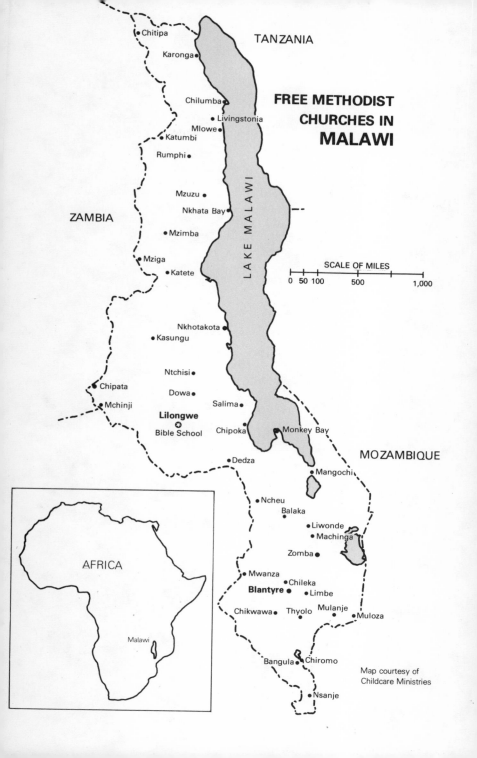

1
Beautiful Feet

What color are "beautiful feet?"

The scripture points out that the feet of those who carry the gospel are "beautiful." Most of us from North America think that beautiful feet are white. Living in Malawi, I've seen some that are black. But some beautiful feet were lobster-red.

She was dying! We had done all we could. We had moved her pastor husband into a more urban setting, so he could be near a hospital for her treatment. But she was dying.

Not sure of the various medical diagnoses she had received from several doctors, we took her to a mission hospital which has excellent medical staff. We stayed with her through the examination. We heard the doctor's pronouncement, "congestive heart failure." He said her life expectancy was short without surgery, and that surgery was not available in Malawi. It might be arranged in South Africa, but there was a limited amount of money for sending patients away for treatment. Only ten or twelve each year can go.

She was too old (about thirty years) to be considered, and by now, it was almost too late. The doctor gave her medication, admonished her not to have any more children, and referred her to a doctor she could see regularly, only a few miles from her home.

Now, just a few weeks later, she lay dying. Her husband came to ask me if he could borrow money to take her to her home before she died. She wanted to be in the circle of her immediate family.

How would he take her? By bus. It was nearly 150 miles and the last fifteen were off the bus route. He said he'd put her on his bicycle, or hire an ox cart to take her as far as possible, then try to find someone to help carry her.

I hadn't seen the woman for a few weeks and really didn't know how seriously ill she was. I told him we'd come the next day in the Bible school pickup, and take her to Lilongwe. They could ride a bus from there.

When we saw her, we knew she would never survive the trip on a bus. She could not even sit up to greet us properly. We carefully placed her on a mattress in the back of the pickup and drove as gently as we could to the Bible school. We found an empty dorm room and made arrangements for her and her husband to be fed and to spend the night.

Phil Capp, southern Africa missionary, was a guest lecturer at the Bible school at the time. He and I left early the next morning with the pastor and his wife in the back of the pickup. We drove to the end of the road, fifteen miles beyond the end of the bus route. We parked the car and made a litter of an old camp cot and two poles and carefully placed her on it. The three of us began to carry her.

As we went along the path, others saw us, recognized the family, and joined in. Soon there were six, then eight, then more. We took turns carrying. The path was one-lane so the journey was not easy, but we made it — until we came to the river.

It was rainy season and the river was running high. We had to cross. There was a place, not too deep. Some of the local men scouted the riverbed to find the best route. Off came our shoes. Up rolled our pant legs. Into the water we went. We certainly looked funny. Four lily-white, soft feet amid the many rock-hard, leathery black ones. But we went on unembarrassed.

When we had crossed the river, we didn't stop to put our shoes on. In fact, we left them behind. We were going to return anyway.

Finally, we arrived at the village, tired, but happy to be there. The family welcomed home the one who was so seriously ill. They took her inside a hut and ministered to her needs. We stayed outside, visited with family members and caught our breath.

Then we looked at our feet. What had been lily-white were now lobster-red. The hot African sun had done its job and the sunburn was thorough.

We recrossed the river, put on our shoes, and drove back to Lilongwe. We really didn't think much about it. Anyone would have done what we did. She was our sister, our pastor's wife, in need. We did what we could.

The pastor's wife died just a few days later and was buried near her home. The pastor went back to his circuit and continued his ministry.

Word spread like wildfire. Two white missionaries had carried a Malawian woman home to die. Who had heard of such a thing? What kind of love is this? The area chief heard the story and said, "This is the church I want here."

We didn't preach. We didn't hand out tracts. We didn't show any films or tell any Bible stories. We simply carried a friend home and prayed with her. Perhaps it was the most significant ministry we have had in Malawi.

What color are beautiful feet? Red? Yellow? Black? White? All are precious in His sight, if they are following in His footsteps.

Malawians on typical rough and rocky trail between villages.

2
Malawi Vignette

A Child Shall Lead Them

Our sons were six and four years old when we first visited Damba Village. They are normal healthy boys. And they are "color-blind." Black kids, white kids, no matter. What *does* matter is *kids*. ("Kids" are boys and girls your own age.)

Anytime we stopped our car we were immediately surrounded by dozens of children, and Damba Village was no exception. Our boys grabbed their Tonka toys and were off for the nearest shade tree. Malawi dirt is perfect for making roads, driving cars, and making all the appropriate sounds. Soon "best friends" were made (even though there was no linguistic communication possible). The Tonka toys began to circulate.

We stayed at Damba for a week. Each night the boys tossed their Tonkas into a box under our VW Camper. The last morning, the toys were gone. The local children didn't know we were coming back four weeks later. But we knew. So we told the local headman what had happened.

When we returned, the headman presented our boys with their toys. As soon as we had left the village, the children had started playing with them.

I watched my boys, wondering what they would do. To my astonishment, they headed for the shade tree and called for their friends. Soon the Tonkas were in full circulation again. I was moved by their total unselfishness. I learned a lesson from my boys.

However, that night the box of Tonka toys went

inside, instead of under the car. A little prevention is wise, and harmless.

Sock Dolls

We sat in the shade of the thatched roof hut, the old superintendent and I. Flies buzzed lazily. Children played in the dirt nearby. It would be two or three hours before the next service. We rested and dozed.

As I saw the children playing, I remembered the black plastic bag stuffed in the back of my car. It was full of "sock dolls," dolls made from men's work socks by women in the United States. This seemed like an opportune moment to distribute them. I didn't have many, and there weren't many children.

I asked the old superintendent what he thought about the idea, and he was 100 percent in favor.

I wandered over to my car, fished out the black plastic bag, and called the children to come near. As I began to hand out the dolls, children "materialized" out of the African bush. Where did they all come from?

Children are delighted with sock dolls.

I kept handing out dolls, and children kept coming, and I kept handing out dolls. I got to the last doll just as I got to the last child. (I have no problem believing in the miracle of the meal and the oil, or the multiplication of the loaves and fishes.)

I put away the empty plastic bag and went back to my chair in the shade. For a while we watched as the children played. Some had found pieces of cloth and were tying their "babies" on their backs. Others were cooking "cornmeal" mud porridge to feed their "babies." The atmosphere was alive with excitement.

The old superintendent turned to me and said in halting English, "The people in America must love very much to give such wonderful gifts to our children whom they have never seen!"

"Inasmuch as you have done it unto one of the least of these . . . you have done it unto me" (Matthew 25:40).

Hospitality Plus

"Breakfast's ready!" The old evangelist was calling our evangelism team.

"Eat a lot of rice porridge," I told them. "We have services in far villages today, and we don't know when we will eat again."

So we ate. It was good!

A half hour later the car was loaded and we were ready to go. The old evangelist came to us and said, "It's time to eat."

"What?" Maybe I misunderstood. I was just beginning to learn Chichewa. "What? We just ate."

"Yes," he replied. "But that was breakfast. This is lunch. We don't know if we will find food at the church where we are going, so we must eat lunch now."

I encouraged the team . . . so we ate. Cornmeal

porridge and boiled chicken. It was good!

Off we went, down the paths, through the fields, until we reached the small mud-plastered church. The bell started clanging as soon as our approaching car could be seen. The tiny church was packed. The service was good.

After the service, the people asked our team to remain in the church. We visited for a while. Then in it came . . . dinner! A dishpan full of delicious boiled rice, cooked to perfection. And boiled chicken, mouth-watering in its gravy. So we ate. And it was good.

About three hours later we pulled back into the old evangelist's village, tired but happy. His wife came out to meet us.

"Dinner's ready," she said brightly. So we ate. Mm-m-m, cornmeal porridge and boiled chicken. It *was* good!

That one day the windows of heaven were opened and blessings — more than we could hold — were poured upon us through God's warm-hearted people in Malawi.

3

The Long Road

Driving in Africa is never boring. There are rare and unique wildlife species to see. Village life and domestic animals are often along the way. Evidences of modern society creep in here and there, like the new car I saw recently under the grass-thatched carport alongside the mud hut. Then, there are the breakdowns. Automotive, that is. Our car has more stories to tell . . .

It all began in 1974 when we came as first-term missionaries to Rhodesia (now Zimbabwe). We bought a secondhand Volkswagen (VW) Camper in South Africa, with only twenty thousand miles on it. It saw rough service and about forty thousand more miles during those next two years. Then came the war in Zimbabwe and we returned to the United States. Our car stayed on in the missionary family. Clifford Guyer drove it for a while, then Clarke DeMille. They took good care of it and changed engines a couple of times and added miles.

When we returned in January 1981, the old car was sitting in Guyers' yard in Johannesburg, still registered in my name. We took it over again.

This time, we lived in Chiredzi, Zimbabwe, where the temperature is about 110 degrees Fahrenheit for six to eight months of the year. To add to that, ethanol made from sugar cane was now added to the petrol (gasoline). Thirty-five percent alcohol makes the petrol burn hotter, and the air-cooled VW couldn't handle it. It melted one of the pistons after only six thousand miles on a new VW engine. The car was in the shop for fourteen weeks while we walked or rode a bicycle.

Finally, it was ready for the road.

We headed south. After four hundred miles, the engine blew up. Clifford and Myrtle Guyer came on Saturday night to meet us and tow us in. I could tell you of the all-night towing, the syphoning of petrol from my car to theirs in the middle of the night, the arrival in Johannesburg just as the sun was coming up the next morning, of the two-hour nap before we headed out to an all-day mine service. But those are just incidentals. We stayed in Johannesburg a week while a new Ford V-6 water-cooled engine was being installed.

What excitement! Double power at the same mileage. And a dependable engine.

Unfortunately, it isn't only the engine that affects how your motorcar operates. Let me tell you some experiences.

There was the time the alternator froze up. With the alternator pulley not turning, there was no way to turn the fan or the water pump. We were one hundred miles from home, or anyplace else, and it was dark. After some unloading, assessing of the problem, and an unofficial committee meeting, we decided to use a pair of my wife's nylon stockings — which she was not wearing at the moment. We ripped the panty hose in two and tied them tightly around the pulleys needed, one each way. We drove fairly slowly, using only low beam lights all the way home. The next morning there was still enough "juice" in the battery to start the car. Now, we always carry a spare pair of panty hose in the toolbox. That way, if my fan belt breaks, or my wife discovers a run, there is a spare.

On another trip, we had a team doing evangelistic work in Malawi for a month. We were about three-fourths done with our tour. The day we were to leave Balaka, we loaded the car. When I got in the car to hitch it to the trailer, the throttle pedal went clear to

Many vehicles carry a full load. Singing youth.

the floor, but the engine just idled. I had broken a cable. I didn't even know it had a cable.

I crawled under the car and discovered the problem. Some time later, I had pulled the cable out of its housing from both ends, rerouted it under the car in the shortest distance possible between the two points, and tied a loop in each end. A piece of baling wire and a little tension on the throttle cable, and the thing was united again, at least temporarily. I cleaned up, and we were off!

A few days earlier we had had a flat tire on the trailer. I put on the spare and found that the flat was caused by the whole valve core coming loose in its rubber casing. I tried to find a replacement tube, but there were none available in Malawi. I used some epoxy putty and stuffed the valve core back into its rubber housing, pumped a low pressure of air into it, and hoped I would never have another flat. Well, I didn't hope hard enough.

Halfway from Balaka to Lilongwe, driving with my wired throttle cable, the trailer had another flat. This time I was unable to jack it as I had before. The VW jack is supposed to fit a little arm into a little hole in the car. The little arm folds down when not in use. How do you put an arm that folds *down* under a trailer box to jack it *up?* My son, Eric, had an idea. Why not put a rock on the ground, set the jack upside down on top of it, and jack the jack down to make the trailer go up. He found the rock, I reversed the jack, and it worked! But would the puttied tube hold? It did! A couple of hours later we slowly and carefully pulled in beside our Lilongwe residence on a wing and several prayers.

The next day, I went to a garage and bought the last throttle cable in Malawi for a VW Camper.

But there were still no tubes. I found a friend who had a car awaiting parts. It had wheels with the same size holes that my trailer needed. My trailer used sixteen-inch wheels, and these were fourteen-inch. So what, if the holes matched? They did, and I towed the trailer to Zimbabwe on his wheels and carried them back to him on the next trip. That was another problem temporarily solved.

The car continued to work for the remainder of our evangelism tour. We headed back to Zimbabwe where we lived. In order to meet our schedule, we had to leave early Sunday morning. We crossed the border into Zambia and headed south. About thirty-five miles from the border, about fifteen miles from Chipata, Zambia, I looked in my mirror. The trailer was dragging its tail. I figured the hitch must have come loose, so carefully slowed down and pulled over to the roadside.

The tongue of the trailer was made from three square hollow steel tubes. The tubes had broken on three sides and just the strap of metal on the bottom of all three was holding the trailer box to the tongue. I gently pushed the trailer box down to level, reloaded the trailer for balance, and slowly and carefully went back to Chipata. There were four hundred miles of bush in front of me. Chipata was our only hope. But on a Sunday morning?

A policeman directed us to a trucking garage where "someone might be." Sure enough, although the manager had been away for several days, he had returned home the night before and had come to his office to see what had happened in his absence. He called a welder and three hours and twenty-one welding rods later, we were on our way again. It didn't look good, but I didn't think it would break.

I noticed grease had been heating up in a trailer wheel bearing, so kept adding more grease to keep it rolling. No bearings in Zambia.

We were finally only one hundred miles from Harare, the capital of Zimbabwe. Feeling good now. It won't be long . . .

Bang! The left front tire of the VW blew out at sixty miles an hour. We stopped safely and changed it.

The next morning in Harare, I set out shopping. We purchased the last tire in stock in our VW size at the National Tyre Company. I bought the last bearing our size at the bearing company, because the trailer bearing was completely shot. That was one of our worst trips for a total of automotive mishaps. But isn't it exciting how the Lord always had an answer for us, and we were able to finish our work?

Recently we had five flat tires on one trip from Malawi to Zimbabwe and back. Once we had two in Zambia on the four-hundred-mile stretch of road. We had to use tire irons and change it the old-fashioned way. We made a boot out of an old tube to cover a rock cut in the tire, and hoped we could make it the next three hundred miles. We did. Somehow, we always do.

After two rebuilds on the Ford engine because of some faulty parts when it was originally assembled, we put in another Ford engine. We had driven only one hundred miles when the car quit running. We had already been delayed a week or more, so we were tired and discouraged.

I thought the problem was electrical. I more or less isolated it to the coil. (Have I learned a lot about cars!) I hitched a ride to a service station about ten miles down the road. The attendant had a coil and sold it to me. I went back, installed it, and the car still wouldn't start.

I hitched a ride back. The attendant wasn't a mechanic; the manager wasn't a mechanic. In fact, he ran a little grocery store attached to the service station. Nevertheless, he accompanied me back, and we puttered and tried this and that for an hour or more. Finally, I dug out an old VW engine coil I had, and we hooked it up. The car started! The chances of buying a faulty coil are small, but I'd done it. The service station manager gave me back my money, and we spent it in his store on lunch and souvenirs. Next town, I bought a spare coil.

One classic story happened when mission board representatives Dr. and Mrs. John Gilmore were visiting southern Africa. Our first four thousand miles had been relatively uneventful. I think it was only one front wheel bearing we had to replace. But as we drove into Lusaka, Zambia, steam belched out of the radiator and over the windshield. The thermostat had stuck and the engine had overheated. No big matter. I now carry spare everything.

I dug out my spare thermostat and removed the old one. We didn't have a gasket, so I had to make one. We reassembled the whole thing and tested it. Water spurted out the side. We took it apart again, redid the gasket, and cranked her down again. But I wasn't too smart. I tightened one side too tight and snapped off the "ear" that is used to bolt the thermostat housing to the engine. Now we were in trouble.

We were planning to leave at 7:00 a.m., but stores didn't open until eight o'clock. We rested well, borrowed a ride into town the next morning, and tramped the streets. We went into every automotive parts place in Lusaka. No such part. "Order it from South Africa," we were told. We finally found an engineering shop which could weld aluminum. For twenty-five dollars, the job was done. (Later I bought a new part in South Africa for about four dollars.)

I paid another ten dollars for gasket cement, and we took a taxi back to our campsite. We couldn't find any more gasket material and hadn't located any in town either, so we used a gasket off an extra radiator cap, cemented it, and carefully reassembled our thermostat. It worked! We drove the next five hundred miles to Lilongwe without further automotive mishap.

A few days later we took the Gilmores to see Lake Malawi. We still hadn't been able to get our new housing from South Africa. Halfway to the lake, the welding sprang a leak. Fortunately for our wives (unfortunately for us), there was a little homemade souvenir stand nearby where a Malawian made and sold ebony carvings.

We cooled the engine and found the leak. We loosened the hose that goes into the thermostat housing. We emptied out enough water so we could dry the inside of the housing. We mixed some epoxy cement and plastered the hole from the inside. A few minutes to dry, hook up the hose, refill the radiator, and we were on our way. We went to the lake, home again, and drove for two more weeks before our new housing came. I still carry in the car that old, welded, epoxied housing. Never know when you'll need something like that!

When I had been in South Africa not long before this, I had seen the mechanic tighten my car's rear wheel bearings — tight. I didn't know any better. So when I got to Lundi Mission (Zimbabwe) again, I tightened down my trailer wheel bearings — tight! They

One of the better roads — but hardly a superhighway!

Pickup trucks don't die — they just rattle away.

were a bit loose. Well, lesson number 5000-something in auto mechanics was about to take place, and it was an expensive, time consuming lesson. You don't tighten trailer wheel bearings the same as car rear wheel bearings.

Six miles from Lundi, fully loaded with our family of four, a Zimbabwean teacher, a South African pastor, one of our Malawian students, and all our luggage, traveling at about sixty-five miles per hour, we lost a trailer wheel. By the time we stopped, the pavement had ground the axle end in half.

We left our sons and the student with the trailer and went back to Lundi. We unloaded, arranged for a friend with a pickup to go for our trailer, went back and unloaded the trailer-load into the car, helped lift the empty trailer onto the pickup, and returned to Lundi. There we called some friends in Chiredzi and arranged for someone to come get the trailer and haul it to Chiredzi (one hundred miles) for repairs. The boys and the student stayed at Lundi while the rest of us finally went on to Harare, arriving at 10:00 p.m. The Zimbabwean teacher had a meeting at eight o'clock the next morning; the South African pastor flew back to Johannesburg, and we returned to Lundi via Chiredzi.

Our friend had been able to machine another axle end to fit our trailer and had obtained bearings. By five o'clock it was finished. It had cost us about three hundred dollars, a six-hundred-mile round trip to Harare, and two days' time.

In December 1985, the old red VW Camper was retired. It had more than 300,000 miles on it. It went out in a blaze of glory. The old engine never skipped a beat on its last trip from Malawi to Zimbabwe where it was to be sold. Over twelve hundred miles with no problems. Didn't seem right, somehow.

But when the new owner bought it and headed for South Africa on vacation, just 250 miles from home the thermostat stuck and the engine overheated. He didn't notice the temperature gauge, so he burned up the engine.

There's a shiny two-tone brown VW Camper in our carport tonight. It has a Ford V-6 engine — brand new. The car only had twenty-five thousand miles on it, and we got a good deal. We only had one flat tire on the way up here with it from Johannesburg. Of course, there was the one-half gallon of Worcestershire sauce that spilled all over the trailer and soaked into twenty-five pounds of laundry soap. But that's another story.

New vehicles were provided for Malawi in January 1986. A pickup for the Bible school, and a camper for Henry and Bonnie Church.

4
This Way to Comfort

The woman's thin plaintive voice came from inside the house ... "This world is not my home, I'm just a-passin' through. . . ." The crowd outside picked up the melody and the words, and the music swelled. There was no handclapping, no rhythmic movement. The song was sung slowly. It was a funeral.

The child's body was inside the house, covered by a cloth. The family and close friends sat nearby. The music continued for hours.

The evening before, the child had died of malarial complications. As soon as the pastor and church people heard about it, they gathered in the home. All night they sang and prayed with the family. The child's family was comforted by their presence and their songs.

As the morning wore on, a crowd gathered. Friends, neighbors, fellow workers, all came to bring their condolences to the family who had lost a child. Then they sat on the ground under the trees, in the shade of the overhanging roof. Sometimes singing, sometimes praying, just being near to lend strength and comfort by their presence. Muslims, Christians, black, white, all sat, and sang.

The coffin was a simple black wooden box made by friends of the family. When it arrived, it was carefully carried into the house by some of those who had been sitting around the home. The Christians kept singing. The family gently placed the body of their young son inside the box, and the lid was nailed on. The Christians continued singing. The box was carefully carried outside and placed on a mat in a clear space in the middle of the crowd of several hundred people. The funeral service began.

In Malawi, the Malawi Congress Party (only political party in the country) is often in charge of funerals. The local party leader began the funeral with the speech of sympathy to the family, and read the long list of names of friends and organizations who had given condolence gifts. (The church had given a basket of cornmeal.) Then the area party chairman spoke in sympathy. He, in turn, introduced the district chairman, who also brought a message of condolence on behalf of himself as well as of the president of the country.

Next, the area chief, an aged Muslim, nearly blind, leaning on the arm of one of his councilors, brought greetings and a message of sympathy. Then the Christians sang again, a hymn of faith. Now, the church was in charge.

Pastor brought a message, not of sympathy as much as of hope. "We are Christians! This world is *not* our home. We are not as those who have no hope. Christ is the Resurrection. In Him we have hope. We will meet our child again."

After the sermon and prayer, the Christians began to sing. Those nearby picked up the small wooden coffin and began to walk. The family followed close behind. Some were crying. The Christians sang. Every few yards someone else would step up and take his place carrying the coffin. Traffic was stopped as the procession of hundreds walked by still singing, led by the Christians of the church. Drivers alighted from their cars and motorbikes and stood respectfully as the procession passed.

The grave had been dug, the usual six feet long, six feet deep, but with an additional space in the bottom, just the size of the coffin. Gently it was lowered into that space. Small poles were put across the top with the child's sleeping mat placed on them, covering the coffin. Then the graveside service was ready to begin.

The Christians sang throughout the service. Once again the party leaders made remarks, and the pastor brought a brief message. Family members sprinkled a handful of dirt into the grave. The women left. The men filled the grave. The service was finished.

There was time to think during the long walk home.

The music brought a quiet peace to the hearts of all who cried. "Blessed are they that mourn, for they shall be comforted." Surely they were comforted by the songs of faith and strength!

Malawi has one of the highest infant mortality rates in the world. Death is no stranger. But it is no welcome friend either. Moms and dads in Malawi hurt just like moms and dads in America or Europe. Color, language, background, make no difference. Death is painful. Christ has a healing balm, and He applies it through the lives of Christians.

When you ask a pastor, "Why does the church grow in Malawi?" one of the answers he will give you is, "Funerals." Funerals? Yes. Our church is a warmhearted, caring church. Our pastors attend funerals, even of children. If there is no other pastor present, ours will preach, pray, and sing. Hurting parents and friends want to know which church it is that has a pastor who cares so much about them. When they find out, they ask, sometimes they beg, for a church to be started in their village.

The church in Malawi is a channel through which the Lord Jesus Christ can pour His healing love into the life of a hurting family.

Children are much loved. They have great fun with simple "toys."

5
Life in Malawi

Traveling Mercies

She was crammed down in the small space between the petrol barrels in the back of a pickup. Her baby was on her lap, with only a thin cloth between it and the wind.

My car was traveling faster. I came up behind the pickup. The woman was unmoving (she probably couldn't), unsmiling, tolerating. We followed the pickup for a mile or so, then around and on we went, never to see the woman again. But I thought about her.

I wondered where she was going. How long had she waited for a ride? How desperate was she that she had to accept these traveling conditions? Did she know the driver or just catch a ride? Was her baby well, or sick? Does she know that Jesus loves her?

Who is she? Just one of nameless people — one face among the masses. But this face had caught my attention and captured my thoughts, and maybe stirred up a bit of compassion from somewhere deep within me.

I can ease into my car and sail along comfortably. I don't like it if I have too many people in my car and feel crowded. I like my "space!"

I go when I want to. I don't have to wait hours — sometimes days — for a thirty-passenger bus, only to find that it is already overloaded.

I jump on my Honda and "zip" to the post office. I don't have to ride a rickety bicycle that should have been retired years ago, tires tied to the rims by pieces of old inner tube.

Things I take for granted are like miracles for other people. I wonder how many other blessings I have that I am so used to that I seldom give thanks.

I had had cornmeal porridge four times in the past twenty-four hours, and I was ready for a change.

I directed my car away from the crowded township where our pastor lives, to the spacious tourist hotel with their "European-style" coffee shop. I ordered a pot of black coffee and a bowl of vanilla ice cream. Mm-m-m.

As I sat and savored the flavor of that delicious substance melting in my mouth and enjoyed a fine cup of coffee, suddenly I realized how easy it is for me to change worlds. Twenty-four hours in an African home, eating good cornmeal porridge, and sharing in their lives. Then across town to a totally different lifestyle, mostly dictated by economics. How easy it is for me to change from one culture to the other. When will my hard-working African pastor-brother ever have a bowl of vanilla ice cream in the hotel? It is a sobering thought!

A beggar sat on the sidewalk in front of the pharmacy. He was obviously disfigured and unable to work. His clothing was threadbare and shabby. He only wanted a few *tambala* (cents).

I passed him by, walked into the pharmacy, and bought some medicine for the skin problem of another missionary's dog. "That's K3.75 (three *kwatcha*, seventy-five *tambala*, or about three dollars), please." I paid the cashier and went on my way. As I walked down the sidewalk, I paused by the poor beggar and gave him 5t (about four cents) from my change. He thanked me with great gratitude. I went on my way feeling good. Then, it hit me . . .

I had spent K3.75 on skin medicine for a dog, and

5t to help a poor beggar. I wonder with which investment Jesus will be the most pleased?

Holey Sox or Sockey Holes

There was a leadership problem in the church that had to be handled carefully. I took another church leader with me and we went into the area where a special meeting was to take place. We didn't want to arrive at the meeting until the following morning, so the church leader and I went to a nearby hotel where we had dinner together and shared a room.

I travel light. That night I washed out my shirt and my socks and hung them over the bath to dry. My roommate observed my behavior and did the same.

The next morning I retrieved my now dry clothes and was dressing when I noticed his socks. I tried to decide whether they should be called "holey socks," or "sockey holes." They were more hole than sock, and from the heel down, they were basically non-existent.

Later, I saw him dressing and trying to arrange these socks so that what was left of them showed, and what wasn't wouldn't be noticeable. I couldn't stand it. I fished around in my bag and came up with an extra pair of my socks. He was very pleased. But he kept his others, too.

Sometimes we are careless and even wasteful. We need to be brought up short to see what someone else's need is and how God wants to use us to meet it.

O God, let me see the faces, sense the pain, understand the needs of people around me. Help me see them as You see them. Forgive my lack of thankfulness for my blessings. Show me how to be a part of Your blessing to them!

Laymen in Luchenza

I had never been to Luchenza.

I had a few days and was visiting as many of the pastors as I could on my way to Salima for a meeting. Arriving in Blantyre, I met with our pastor. I told him I'd also like to visit Luchenza, though the pastor there didn't know I was coming.

Off we went in high hopes. It was a lovely drive, and a beautiful Malawi day.

The pastor at Luchenza was absolutely dumbfounded. He had never dreamed that I would visit him. And here I was, totally unexpected.

He invited the Blantyre pastor and me into the house. There we met two laymen. We spent some time in exchanging greetings and news with typical Malawian hospitality.

"Do you know these men?" the pastor then asked me. I didn't, as far as I could remember.

"These are two of my laymen from the Zomba area. Their home is eighty miles from here. They came by foot for me to teach them some Bible lessons, so they can go back and teach their churches. Since I can't get to Zomba often, each month they come here for two days of lessons."

Now it was my turn to be astounded. Eighty miles! By foot! To learn a lesson to teach others. I remembered some of my U.S.A. experiences when it was often hard to get people to drive a few blocks for a training class.

The men didn't think of the eighty-mile walk as anything terribly unusual. They had left at evening in order to avoid the heat and had walked all night and all the next day, arriving at Luchenza in the evening. The following evening they would start home.

I was challenged, burdened, convicted, thrilled, all

at the same time. What a conflict of emotions these men stirred within me!

Their church in Zomba was started five years before when a teacher and Bible school students, during a brief stop, held one afternoon service under a tree. We sometimes had wondered if those services really did any good. If you wonder, ask two laymen in Luchenza.

Zipatso Jam

Rice three times a day didn't bother us. We had rice porridge for breakfast, rice and gravy for lunch, and gravy and rice for dinner. Malawian women can cook rice to perfection. So we ate it and enjoyed it.

We had been in Malawi about three weeks, having never missed a meal of rice, when we were invited to lunch in one of the villages where we were staying. We called to our sons and told them, "Wash up! It's time to eat!"

As the boys came running, the oldest panted out, "Oh boy! I hope we have rice!" He was serious. He loved rice. And he got his wish.

But even if you like rice as much as we did, a change of diet is really a treat.

Each evening after the kids were asleep in the camper and the students and church leaders were off to their lodgings, we'd have a "staff meeting." That meant that Bonnie and I and Elesinah Chauke and Phil Capp, the staff on this tour, would meet in our camper for tea or coffee and toast. Toast never tasted so good. We could get margarine in small tins, and bread was usually available in the small trading stores. We feasted late every night.

One day Phil and I were in a small store and Phil said, "Let's get some jam for our staff meeting tonight." There was a whole shelf of jam. A real treasure trove.

Phil picked up a tin of "Mixed Fruit Jam" and said, "How about this?" The price was reasonable.

But I had spied the local Malawi label. They had strawberry! "Phil!" I cried, "Let's really splurge! Let's get some strawberry jam."

We could hardly wait until our services were over, the kids in bed, the students on their own, so we could produce our surprise. The coffee and tea were brewed, the toast made. Out came our prize — real strawberry jam.

As we opened the tin, the smell was enough to stimulate our salivary glands. We took a bite, and looked at one another in mid-chew. Phil picked up the tin, and for the first time read the contents listed on the label: "Strawberry Flavored Zipatso Jam. Made from mangos, pineapples, paw-paws, and pumpkin."

We hadn't wanted mixed fruit. So we paid extra for mixed fruit — and vegetables. Next stop we bought a chocolate bar. Now, that *was* a splurge!

Surprises may await the traveler who ventures into a general store in Malawi.

6
Clinic

Today was my first time to take a blood pressure. Well, I did take my wife's a few times to practice. Nearly squeezed her arm off at 200 before I realized it didn't need to go above 140. But today it was "for real."

Some months ago we took the wife of one of our students to a mission hospital where we had confidence in the doctors. She had been sick for two years. Nothing had seemed to help. But she only saw a medical assistant who didn't even take her blood pressure.

I decided something should be done. I bought a sphygmomanometer and a stethoscope and had a lesson from Dr. Leif Brauteseth, son of Free Methodist missionaries in South Africa. Then I was ready.

Twenty women arrived two days ago for the module for students' wives. The first day there was a group of "sniffy noses" and headaches. No problem.

This morning, a young mother told me, "It's my heart!" I asked her to come back after class, and I dug out my equipment. This afternoon she came, she and a friend. Out came the cuff and stethoscope. Very professionally done, it was. Blood pressure, 120 over 75 or so. Pulse, 72 and strong. Sorry, lady, no *mankwala* (medicine) for you.

The friend also had "heart." By now there were six more women sitting on the floor of the office, waiting their turn. This one had 125 over 80. Pulse, 95. Hm-m-m. Why? What should I do? All I've ever had is Red Cross First Aid I. I asked her what she had been doing. "Carrying water?"

"No."

"Running or walking?"

"No."

"What?"

"Sitting."

"Oh! Hm-m-m. How have you been feeling otherwise?"

"I am having malaria."

"Oh. Then you have been feeling hot with fever?"

"Yes."

Now I saw it. I gave her two aspirin to take now and two for tonight for her fever. Her heart is fine. "Next!"

A succession of patients came in. There was a baby with a stuffy nose. Baby aspirin was all I had. Then a mother with a stuffed nose. How about some antihistamine? Stomach pain? Try Tums. Headache is easy. Good old aspirin. Our clinic couldn't function without antimalarials, aspirin, and Tums.

One lady had poked a stick into her foot and had an infection. Out came the hydrogen peroxide to clean it, a bit of antibiotic ointment, and a bandage. (Bless the women's group in the U.S. that sent that roll of bandages.)

A child had ringworm. I recognized it from the time one of us had it, and I used the medicine left over from our treatment.

There were three or four more hearts to listen to (one had very low blood pressure) and a couple who self-diagnosed their problem as "no blood." As a final prescription, I found a bottle of multiple vitamins which had come in a care package and gave them to the student captain to dispense, one a day per student.

Another day a woman came to the office saying she had heart trouble. I took her blood pressure and got 130 over 70 or so, and gave her antacid. A few days later she was back. She said she had malaria and heart. She did have a temperature, so I gave her antimalarial tablets, then told her her heart was fine.

Being principal of a Bible school calls for skills not offered in the normal ministerial training program at Seattle Pacific University. But healthy students learn better. So little knowledge, so few supplies have to go so far to help so many.

With a few simple remedies Henry Church alleviates illness, pain, and anxiety.

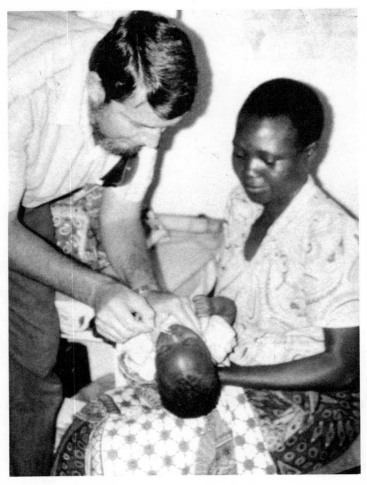

The needs of Bible school students and their families are met at the school clinic.

7
Letter from a Student

The following letter was received from a student in the Malawi Bible School one month after the first women's module which his wife had attended. The wives of our students attend one two-week module each year.

His father had just died, and we had sent a small offering as a condolence. His letter reads:

Beloved:

I have accepted your condolence and encouragements, and I thank the Lord for the oneness that

Student wives at Malawi Bible School

exists among the children of God. That has assured me that I was not alone during my dark hour. Praise the Lord!

The second point is this, I must thank the Lord again for arranging the 1986 women's module. Do you know how it has helped me?

We have been married for thirty-one years and since that time, our marriage meant nothing. My wife was a separate person; she didn't belong to me, and I'm sure I didn't belong to her.

She could oppose everything that I said and did; she could not cooperate with me on anything.

Since she returned from the Bible school she has completely changed. She is a lovable woman. I wished if she could come here much earlier. We are now on a honeymoon. Praise the Lord for guiding you in His work.

May God bless you.

Your brother,
(signature)

There are times of weariness, but these kinds of responses rejuvenate and motivate. The job is being done. Some lives are changed. Thank God!

8

Malawi Theological Education

The Free Methodist Church in Malawi is the result of a theological education program — in Zimbabwe.

A Malawian was working in the sugar fields of Zimbabwe (then Rhodesia), in 1969, when he became truly converted. He heard of the Free Methodist Bible School at Lundi Mission and went there to apply for admission.

Even though he wasn't a Free Methodist, the rules were bent a little, and he was allowed to enroll, provided he would return to Malawi and bring his wife and family to the Bible school as well. He did so, and worked his way through Lundi Bible School.

Shortly before his graduation, when he was deciding where to go and what to do with his new knowledge, the Lord appeared to him in a series of dreams and told him to return to his homeland and plant the seeds of the Free Methodist Church. In obedience to these dreams or visions, he left his church and joined the Free Methodists. Soon he was graduated and returned to Malawi.

It was only a matter of weeks before more applications began coming to Lundi Bible School from his converts. Could they come and be trained as leaders for the fledgling church? Ultimately, eight students were admitted and made their way, along with their families, to Lundi Bible School.

Before these students could finish their education, the Rhodesia (Zimbabwe) independence war began, and in late 1976 the Malawians were evacuated back to Malawi. Through the next few years a number of missionaries arrived in Malawi to teach short terms to help these students finish their program.

An old store building was bought from an Indian family in Salima. There were rooms in the back that could house students, teachers, classroom, and so forth. It became the church headquarters for a few years. One student returned to his former church, but the rest persisted, planting Free Methodist churches in the process. Finally, they were all admitted into the conference. (Five of those men are still serving in 1986 as conference superintendents, and one is a local deacon.)

Now more students were applying. A new program was instituted, with missionaries Warren and Jean Johnson in charge. They lived in South Africa and commuted to Malawi to stay weeks at a time to train the new students.

Although a few students were lost along the way, there were four students in the program when the Johnsons were officially appointed to Malawi, where they rented a house in Lilongwe, the new capital city of Malawi. Lilongwe is the center of activity now, with good rail, road, and air transport. And it has a cooler climate than Salima.

Small buildings were rented for student accommodation, and Johnsons held class in their living room. Warren Johnson also spent time with officials of the city, looking for the right place as a permanent site for the Bible school.

Unexpected problems arose, and the Johnsons were urgently needed at home. Arrangements were made for me to care for the rent and other business matters by long distance until they returned.

Regularly, I made trips from Zimbabwe, where we were stationed, to Malawi. Sometimes they would be for only a few days, to care for the urgent matters. Sometimes we would extend the trips for evangelism.

Always the question was the same — When will the Bible school reopen?

The students were about halfway through their program, not far enough along to enter the conference as ministerial candidates. Because of a number of complications, Johnsons were unable to return. Months passed by. The question was still there, in my mind and in those of the students.

In late June 1982, I invited Philip Capp to join me in Malawi. I was hoping to organize some classes to get these four students through, or at least keep them busy until Johnsons could return. Philip Capp had been the principal at Lundi Bible School and knew the Malawi situation well. He was now the principal of the Evangelical Bible Seminary of Southern Africa in Pietermaritzburg, South Africa, and one of the foremost authorities on church growth principles in the area.

We brainstormed. We wrote. We rewrote. We got ideas, and then threw them away and started over. What we ended up with after several long days was a new concept of theological education. We were so excited that we even phoned the mission board to discuss our ideas with our denominational leaders.

Receiving preliminary permission to go ahead, we contacted government officials and signed the lease on the property Warren Johnson had found, just a few hundred feet from the house he had rented. Four and one-half acres of prime land in the middle of Chilende Township, Lilongwe. We consulted an architect and a builder and sketched building plans. We wrote up a detailed draft of the program and mailed it to the mission board.

A week had passed and a lot of work had been done. The seeds had been planted, fertilized, and watered for the speedy growth of the Bible school program for Malawi. Philip Capp returned to South Africa, and I met a Missions Adventure Tour group and proudly showed them our weedy, rocky, empty hillside "campus."

The Commission on Missions officially approved the Malawi Theological Education Program at their next meeting. Funds were released. The Salima property was put up for sale. In September 1982, the first shovel of earth was turned, and a single classroom unit was under construction. Shortly, a dormitory began to take shape. Easter of 1983, the Lilongwe congregation met in the classroom that was to be their church sanctuary for the next two years.

Lilongwe used classroom as church sanctuary for two years. Bonnie Church in group at left; Bishop Clyde Van Valin and Luis Wanela on porch.

Word spread and soon we had a number of applications for the Bible school. Eight were admitted in addition to the four who were partly finished. Our first session was scheduled to open in early September 1983. Enrollment: twelve.

The program was designed to develop church-planting leadership for the Malawi church. Only students who are recognized by their pastors and local churches as potential leaders, having demonstrated leadership at the local level, are admitted.

The students attend intensive four-week modules, then return to their homes and churches. We schedule three to four modules for men each year, and one shorter one for women. The modules consist of two to three subjects only. They are taught in English, the business language of Malawi, for most students have a working knowledge of it by the time they are in eighth grade.

We have had no resident staff until recently (January 1986) when we took up residence here. Our program enables other missionaries and volunteer personnel to come for a month and make a significant contribution to the students' education.

Our faculty has included Ph.D.s, pastors from the U.S.A., Free Methodist missionaries from South Africa, Zimbabwean women's leaders and nursing staff, guest lecturers from the Church of the Nazarene and Dutch Reformed Mission. We are able to get the best qualified for the subjects at the least expense. To have all these people resident here would be an extreme financial burden. But we have them for teachers for our program.

Between modules, our students have required scripture memorization to do, and they have home study in assigned Theological Education by Extension (TEE) texts. They also have to work in a local church. Their pastors serve as teachers, sending regular reports to the school on their progress in the field. They also must plant a church each year. Although they are in school only three or four months, they are busy all year.

Our current student body (March 1986) is twenty-seven. Of those, four are the seniors who started under the Johnsons. They graduate at annual conference time, July 1986. They are all ordained deacons. Eight more of them are ministerial candidates and preparatory members of the conference. Some are serving as supply pastors. Fourteen of our students are serving churches under conference appointment.

The program is working. Our students are excited. Every guest lecturer who has been here is excited. Other missions are coming to see our program, and some are interested in using its concepts in their own churches.

Our property has developed. We now have, in addition to the original classroom and dormitory, a second dormitory and dining room. We can accommodate forty students, two to a room. A spacious library has been added, as well as two small offices, a small shop for supplies, a missionary house, a three-room "cabin" completely outfitted for guest lecturers, a pastor's house and appropriate outbuildings, and our church.

The church building was officially opened on May 12, 1985. It was dedicated on September 8, 1985, along with the entire complex, by our new director of missions, Elmore Clyde. The property, now fenced and landscaped, is a credit to our church.

The Department of World Missions of our denomination has evangelism, church planting, and the training of national leadership as stated priorities. The Malawi Theological Education Program is meeting the priority call of Free Methodist missions worldwide.

Elmore Clyde, director of world missions, cuts the ribbon at the dedication of the Lilongwe church.

Theological students relax with a game.

VISA (Volunteers in Service Abroad) teacher Wayne Sawyer at Malawi Bible School.

Malawi Bible School dormitory and kitchen.

9

Comedy of Errors

I always like to be on time for a plane. However, on my first trip to Malawi in several years, I arrived at the Harare (Zimbabwe) airport a full hour before flight time, just in time to see the Air Malawi flight lift off the end of the runway. Do you know the feeling?

In those days there were several flights each week from Harare to Blantyre. Checking at the office, I found that there was another flight leaving Harare at 10:00 p.m. the same day. I decided to take that one.

It would now be necessary for me to spend the night in Blantyre as there would be no connecting flight to Lilongwe until the next day. The airlines booked me and cabled ahead to the Ryalls Hotel for a room. It was all confirmed. That night I was at the airport two hours early, just in case.

The flight left a half hour early with only six passengers on a one-hundred-passenger jet. After arrival and the usual immigration and customs formalities, I caught the last airport bus into town.

Since I had no Malawi *kwatcha* (similar to the U.S. dollar), I could not pay the bus. The driver didn't want a traveler's check. So he stopped at the Mount Soche Hotel, where after some discussion the staff agreed to cash my traveler's check. I paid the driver and on we went to the Ryalls. Unfortunately, the Ryalls had never heard of me and had no booking, and was full!

I picked up my suitcase and tramped the two blocks or so back to the Mount Soche with only a small hope in my heart. Yes, there was a room. Pay in advance for bed and breakfast, even though I had to leave before breakfast to catch my Lilongwe connection. So be it. 12:30 p.m. A bed for a weary body.

Up at 5:00 a.m., and off for Lilongwe. I expected to rent a car at the Lilongwe airport and drive to Salima where I was to meet the church leaders. I knew that the Lilongwe pastor had been to the airport to meet me the day before, but as I hadn't arrived, he wouldn't know when to expect me next. I got off the plane, full of confidence.

"What, no cars?" I was incredulous. I tried both agencies. Someone suggested I call the downtown office. The pay phone was out of order. I borrowed a phone from an office. "No, sir, I'm sorry. All our cars are booked today." What was I going to do?

I went out to catch the airport bus, but it had already left. There would not be another for hours. I sat on a rock, wondering, and asking God what He had in mind anyway.

Soon a Landrover came into the parking lot, and a young man went into the terminal on business. When he came out, I asked, "Please, sir! Are you going into Lilongwe? Could I beg a ride?" His affirmative answer was music to my ears, and away we bumped and rattled.

As we came into town I saw a car rental agency and asked to be dropped there. Upon questioning, I found that all cars were booked, but one would be in by 10:00 a.m. I reserved it!

Across the street was the Old Lilongwe Hotel. What an inviting sight. I walked over and got a *big* breakfast. Afterwards I decided to try to phone the house where our pastor stayed. Unfortunately, he wasn't home. No one in his family spoke English, and I, no Chichewa. Somehow they understood who I was, and that finished that — I thought.

At 10:00 a.m. I went to the car hire agency and was busy filling out forms for the rental. I heard my name. There was the pastor.

"How did you find me?"

"I returned home shortly after your call. My daughter told me you had called. I thought, *If I had just come to town, where would I go?* I knew you would need a car, so I came here."

I took the pastor to his house, and we shared in fellowship and tea. Then I went on my way, uplifted, knowing that the Lord knew the entire program before I ever left home.

I have learned to leave things in His hands, but I do get to the airport earlier.

Wilderness Road

The road was terrible! Impassable! Actually, it wasn't a road at all, just a dry creek bed part of the way, and a path the rest.

As our VW rose and fell with sickening clunks, thunks, and crashes, I mumbled to my wife out of the side of my mouth, "This road? It isn't a road! These people think if you can ride a bicycle someplace, a car can go as well. They don't understand . . ."

I grumbled quietly because our evangelism team and the local pastor were in the back, but I was upset.

When we got there, we hadn't arrived. The village and church were still nearly two miles away, on a path even a bicycle couldn't negotiate. So we walked.

The crowd at the little thatch and mud church was beginning to thin. The people had expected us four hours earlier. But when they saw us coming, they ran to meet us on the path and sang and danced us to the church.

The place was packed. The service was joyful and Spirit-filled. Excitement and enthusiasm were high. We received gratefully a gift of a dozen oranges.

Back along the path we walked. Down the bumpy road we drove to our next service. We would never forget Sanga (Wilderness) Church.

Three days later we were to leave this pastor and his district of several churches. The trailer was hitched, the car packed. The pastor called us into his home for a "farewell." We had some warm Cokes and parting words.

The pastor stood and said, "You missionaries are special to us. You are different from some others. Why, just the other day you drove to Sanga. Now, that road to Sanga wasn't very good. It was hard for your car. But you went, and you didn't even complain."

O God, how often do I say or do the wrong thing. Help me in words, thoughts, and actions, to demonstrate Your love to all.

10
A Sunday Off

Here I sit, just a few feet from the lapping edge of Lake Malawi. It's been a four-day vacation which ends tomorrow morning.

Today is Sunday. We thought we'd drop in on one of our rural churches for our worship service.

They weren't expecting us, and we didn't know if we could locate the place. It had been too long since we had been there. Gwengwe is under one of our students, so we were interested in what we might find.

It's the rainy season. We didn't know how the roads would be. They were passable! We didn't recognize the church. In fact, it wasn't there. Rains and white ants had taken their toll, and the church was just a pile of rubble. Some new poles were tied together with a thatch roof on top. I could see people inside the pole structure, sort of like looking at moving parts inside a skeleton.

Did I say the church was just a "pile of rubble"? What a mistake! The *church* was alive and well. It was only an old building that was rubble. There was *life* in those new "bones."

We were warmly welcomed by the layleader and shown to special seats in the front of the congregation of about forty people. The leader began the service with a speech of welcome saying they had not expected us, and this was an "emergency" to them. We were asked to sing and bring greetings, which we did with great joy and halting speech.

The layleader prayed, then asked . . . "Please . . . ?"

I had figured I'd have to preach so came prepared. But I was counting on the student pastor to interpret, and he wasn't there. The layleader offered his services, and the meeting continued. The Lord blessed. The people were encouraged. We were, too.

While visiting after the service, I asked about our student pastor. "Oh, he's at another church about three or four miles from here. Want to go?"

Our layleader guide jumped into the car, and we bounced on to the next stop, Chitawa church. We'd never been there before.

We could see the service was in progress, and the small church was packed (about seventy-five people). I think the pastor stopped mid-sentence — certainly mid-sermon.

A layman stood to lead a chorus while the pastor came to welcome us and usher us inside. When the chorus was finished, the pastor digressed from his sermon to preach another one . . .

"Jesus said, 'Be ready. In an hour you know not, I'll come!' Our principal has given us an example of that. We didn't know he was coming. No notice. But, here he is, and we're ready to receive him." After further elaboration, he finished his original sermon.

Introductions, greetings, and two special songs by "the principal and the woman of his house," then we had the benediction.

We took the student pastor and his family to their home after church. Also, we still had our layman guide, who had acquired a bicycle from somewhere. We drove down pathways where the grass was taller than the pickup, and the way could only be discerned by the rows of corn growing on either side.

A visit in the shade. Meet all the in-laws. A brief rest. A gift of a live chicken. Then we were on our way back to the lake (via Gwengwe where our layman guide and his bicycle disembarked with appropriate ceremony).

Now, our late lunch is over. Dishes are done. The lake is lapping gently. And I'm thinking . . .

Our unsalaried student pastor, who is in charge of four churches, will visit a nearby chief this Wednesday to see if he can start a church in the chief's village. He'll do it! His churches were organized. Someone was in charge. The people were there. The program was planned. God was there.

We can teach some things in the Bible school. We can plan and produce leadership seminars and workshops. But the training is empty unless energized by the power of the Spirit of God.

Today we saw our teachings bearing fruit because of that energizing power.

A new Free Methodist church in Malawi attracts an overflow congregation.

11

Preacher in Tennis Shoes

There are four bullet holes in the pulpit. The red-orange light of the flickering homemade lamp shines bronze on the preacher's face. He paces to and fro on the platform, forcefully expounding the Scriptures to the sizable congregation.

It is Good Friday evening at Chikombedzi Mission in Zimbabwe. A missionary is there — an unusual occurrence in the last few years. A terrible war has come and gone, leaving its grim reminders. Lives have been scarred and broken, and some lost.

It is a new day for Zimbabwe, a nation celebrating its first anniversary of independence this Easter. Brand new Zimbabwe dollars were printed and distributed this week. There is new rhetoric in the newspapers. So much is new!

But as the missionary strains his limited Shangaan to hear this Good Friday preacher, he hears the old, old story once again.

"Jesus loves us. He suffered for us. He understands our suffering. He prays for us. He gave Himself totally for us. His death is a demonstration of how far He will go — for us."

The bullet holes, broken windows, people who aren't there, the strong words of scripture, joyful music, the full church, all combine to bring power to the closing chorus, "Jesus Is So Wonderful!"

Often back home, we get caught up with our Easter bunnies and bonnets and hot cross buns. We sometimes forget it is Jesus who is so wonderful.

These people couldn't depend on the missionaries

— they weren't there. They couldn't depend on the government — it was at war. They sometimes couldn't even depend on each other — they didn't know whom to trust. But they knew a Friend. He is closer than a brother. He has not failed them!

The preacher did not talk of theory or theology. He spoke with conviction of reality. He wasn't concerned that he had tennis shoes instead of Florsheims. He probably didn't know about hot cross buns. The only thing his Easter bunny is good for is to be eaten with porridge. But he knows whom he has believed, and he is persuaded and has proved during the past five years, that He is able to keep that which is committed to Him!

These people are not waiting for Easter for Jesus to arise. They know He has been alive all the time.

*　　*　　*

Organizational meeting of the WMFI at Lilongwe, Malawi, in May 1986.

12
Red Tape

It began with the purchase of a washing machine and an electric range for our mission house in Malawi.

We knew that as new immigrants we must own something for six months before we could import it duty free. Because we knew that we would be applying for Malawi residence permits, we hurried and bought a washing machine and electric range which we would be needing. We stored them away in a missionary's garage in Johannesburg.

The residence permits were granted nine months after we had made our purchases. We contacted a shipping agency to pick up the washer and stove and transport them to Malawi. The agency agreed and handled the paperwork on their end. The easy part was done.

We received a phone call a few days later. "Your washer and cooker are on the way. They should be in Malawi tomorrow. The following are the truck and container numbers. . . ."

We waited, with no small amount of excitement, until the next day. Then I phoned the local freight handler.

He took my numbers and information and said he would call me back. He didn't. That was on Wednesday. On Thursday, I called again. He was "out." Someone else took my information and told me he was sorry, but that shipment had mistakenly been sent to Blantyre (two hundred fifty miles south). He suggested I should call on Monday.

Monday, I tried again. The freight handler took

down the facts once more. I explained our immigration status again and that we had two crates from within a container. I gave him all the details. He said he would check with customs and see if the goods could be released. "Please call back tomorrow morning."

Tuesday, I gave him until mid-morning. When I called, he had "just sent someone to customs to see if the shipment could be released." He would call back.

He did! I could hardly believe it. He told me that customs had approved and that I could come get the shipment, but to bring a check for K1665.50 (more than one thousand dollars). I was flabbergasted! I asked what the check was for, since we were new immigrants and qualified for the duty-free import of personal items. He said, "Chairs do not qualify for duty-free rebate."

"Chairs!" I nearly exploded. "We don't have chairs. We have a washer and cooker."

"Sorry, sir. No washer and cooker here."

I told him I'd be in touch and hung up.

I phoned the shippers and told them the problem. They said that my stuff was there. They had had the same problem with the freight handler the day before. They would call him and straighten it out.

A few minutes later, the freight handler called me (his second phone call) and said my freight was there, but as no papers had come, there seemed to be a problem. Could I please come to his office. I agreed.

I no sooner had hung up than the shipper called me and told me the freight was *there*. I told them about the "no papers" problem, and they said the shipment couldn't have been received without papers.

I drove several miles to the handler's office. I greeted him and showed him my immigration permit. He was surprised and began to fill out new forms, since I was a new immigrant. He said, "Then, you'll be able to get your freight duty free!" I was speechless. What had I been telling him for days!

After typing several copies of documents, he said, "Let's go to customs to see if we can clear this freight." (I thought that had been done.) I took him in my car to customs, and there he obtained the necessary stamps, and so forth, and we returned to his office.

Now, all that remained to be done was to pay my bill, load my freight, and be on my way. I couldn't believe the size of the bill. For one thing, two dollars for phone calls. I paid the bill, but explained to the finance manager why I was unhappy with his company's services.

Soon the washer and cooker were loaded, and by the end of the day both were installed and operating in our house.

I was lucky. It only took a week and one trip to the freight handling office to clear my freight. Sometimes it really takes time!

Recently I got the licenses for our new car and trailer. Usually it takes about four months. I found a shortcut since we were to leave for Zimbabwe, and we had only been in the country two months. I literally made twenty-one stops at seven different offices all over town before the process was completed. It cost me six stops to hurry the process!

One office takes your money and gives you a receipt which you take to another office, who gives you a number, which you take to a retailer who custom-makes a license plate, which you take back to show office number two so they will stamp your paper, so you can go to the insurance company to change your registration number on its records, so you can return to office number one to pay your fee for this year's license tag.

And all of that doesn't include the customs clearances, duties, bank papers, and police clearances for your funds and later for your vehicle. It is incredibly complicated. But I got the licenses — just hours before we were to leave on our next trip.

Things are different in every country. Customs need to be learned and followed. But even in the warm heart of Africa, one can get frustrated.

When you pray for missionaries, pray for more than their evangelistic opportunities and spiritual ministries. Pray also for their patience and frustration level.

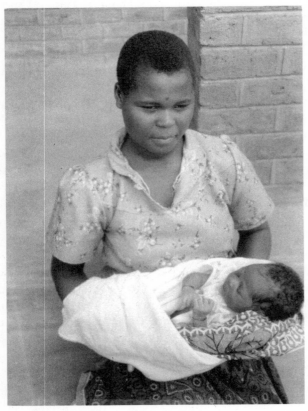

Banda and baby. (See next chapter.)

13
Banda's Baby

"The lady is sick! She is feeling pains. She wants to go to the hospital."

I've heard it all before. Tomorrow, classes will begin for the wives of the Bible school students. Some of them have traveled many miles. Perhaps they hadn't eaten on the way. Perhaps they have motion sickness from the long bus ride. Perhaps only weariness. I have just the thing, Tums. Fixes them up every time.

"I'll go see the lady, Mother. Perhaps I can give her something and she won't need to go to the hospital." I start down the path.

"Wait, teacher! You don't understand. The lady is pregnant. She is feeling pains. She wants to go to the hospital to 'give a baby!'"

"What?" That stopped me in my tracks. "Give a baby?" Tums wouldn't help that. I reorganized.

We loaded the expectant mother and two friends into the pickup and headed for the hospital.

I hadn't even known that this lady had arrived at the Bible school. I hadn't seen her in a year and didn't know she was pregnant. But she was! There we were, on our way to the hospital with an imminent delivery in the back of the pickup.

I really hadn't expected Banda to come to this session of Bible school. You see, her two-year-old daughter had died only five days before. *Five days ago!*

What is it like to be a Bible school student in Malawi?

The average student is about thirty-three years old.

He has about eight years of public school education. That means he has at least a basic background in English but not enough to qualify him for an important job. Perhaps he is one of the 95 percent of the students who are subsistence-level farmers, living in constant debt on the brink of poverty.

As a student he is committed to leadership in the church. Since more than half of the students are appointed as "supply" pastors by the annual conference, he may be one. As required of all students, he works in leadership at the local church level. He must be actively involved in church planting. He may have to relocate from his home in order to serve the church. He probably has so few earthly possessions that he could move them in a wheelbarrow.

What makes the Malawi student outstanding is his level of commitment to Christ and the church. Other jobs may pay more. Other positions provide more prestige. But these men are dedicated to carry out a "call" which comes from beyond themselves.

A grieving mother, only days from death, only hours from new life, riding on an uncomfortably crowded bus to come to a two-week session of Bible school, is an example of the level of commitment of students of our church in Malawi.

(Note: Thirty minutes after arriving at the hospital, the woman gave birth to a beautiful, healthy baby boy. His name is Comfort.)

14
A Big Mistake

Something was wrong! I couldn't put my finger on it, but something was wrong.

We were sitting in the living room of the mission house, the entire conference board of trustees and I. We were discussing the new Bible school buildings which were in progress, the first ones to be built on our site.

Our discussion was all on little items I'd call nit-picking. Little questions about non-essentials. Why? What was the hidden agenda?

Several weeks before, I had secured mission board permission to proceed with the building plans. The architect had drawn the plans, and since I was touring the conference at the time, I took the plans along and showed them personally to each trustee. I explained the program and how the buildings related to the program. I explained the differences between city construction regulations (water-borne sewage, for example) and those of the outlying villages. I explained materials, costs, and so forth. I wanted to be sure they all understood. Every one of them agreed we should go ahead with the building. They were all solidly supportive.

Construction had begun. Things were progressing at the site. The classroom was fairly well up and the dormitory had the foundation in. But things were *not* progressing well at the board meeting. Why?

Suddenly, the light dawned. I interrupted the discussions:

"Gentlemen, I have an apology to make. I see that

I have made a mistake. Please forgive me. I met with you one by one, then went ahead on the buildings without having a committee meeting where we could all get together to discuss. I am so sorry."

Instantly the chairman jumped to his feet, pointed his finger at me and said, "You're right! You made a mistake!" Then in a softer voice, "But we all make mistakes."

Another pastor jumped to his feet and began singing, "Praise the Lord, Allelujah, Amen. Praise the Lord, Allelujah, Amen. Praise the Lord . . ." Everyone got up, clapping and singing, hugging one another and shaking my hand.

At the end of the song, we all sat down and the chairman said, "Now, what's the next item of business?" And that was the end of the matter.

Thank the Lord for the warmhearted people of Malawi who are willing to overlook and forgive the mistakes of a missionary who doesn't always understand their ways.

15
Words of Thanks

Do you ever wonder if you do anything right? Well, I do! When you're working cross-culturally, it is even more difficult to know if you have done well or not. Sometimes you make a mistake and find out about it. Sometimes you succeed and find out about it. Take for example, one of my prized possessions. This letter recently came in the post, and I quote it exactly as it was written. [The GMB is our missions board]:

Dear Principal,

Even though I am too late to write this letter off to you, the GMB, and to the Almighty God, anyway receive it.

I feel much pleasure to thank you & GMB for the great work you have done since I became a student in 1979 to 86 and have a diploma in theology studies.

It's a big job to take care of someone for a long time like this. There are times that we were making some mistakes — still you forgave me. The GMB lost much money so that I must succeed and get this diploma, and also what I want you to know is that not only in class that I was learning but even outside when your wife was busy taking care of everything and also weeding in the flower garden, also yourself carrying heavy goods cutting pipes and also your children making themselves busy. I learned a lesson that my family must be busy working to make our family strong and have improvement in our family because of all these that

I have learned from you and your family. I have gained much and my family now is as it is. Thank you and may God bless you.

Lastly I will never never forget the great job you have done to our family.

Taking care someone's family for so long like that it's not play. Yes, I have succeeded and got this diploma *but* I need to ask myself, Am I going to inherit the Kingdom of heaven or not. Otherwise my diploma can be nothing if I don't think better.

> It is me,
> (First graduate of the
> Theological Education
> Program in Malawi)

Wow!! That's better than a raise in pay!!

*   *   *

There was the time our two sons were playing soccer with a neighborhood full of kids. They were playing on the Bible school property, near where we had just installed a horseshoe pit for the students' recreation. One of the soccer "stars" ran into the horseshoe goal, a piece of pipe sticking about eighteen inches out of the ground. He split his leg wide open.

Dad was called for his first-aid expertise, and the wound was soon disinfected and dressed. But it looked to me like it needed stitches. I was worried. What would the boy's parents think? Would I be in trouble? Would it cause a problem in the neighborhood? Back home, people are sued for less.

The boy's father was not at home, but the mother

came. I explained what had happened (and so did all three dozen of the other soccer players). I told her I thought the boy needed stitches. She didn't know what to do, so I offered to take her and the boy to the hospital. This I did, and I waited and watched the suturing, paid the minimal fee, and took them home again.

The next day I visited the boy in the morning. His pain and agony of the previous day were forgotten. He was now the hero.

In the afternoon I got a letter from his father. He had sent it to our local pastor who gave it to me:

Dear Reverend Pastor,

Will you please on behalf of I personally and my family as a whole convey our heartiful thanks to Reverend H. Church for the heartiful and perfect good hospitality he had shown yesterday; as my son who was hurt was immediately sent to the hospital yesterday.

May the Almighty Lord Bless.

Yours Sincerely,

It sure feels good to do something right once in a while!

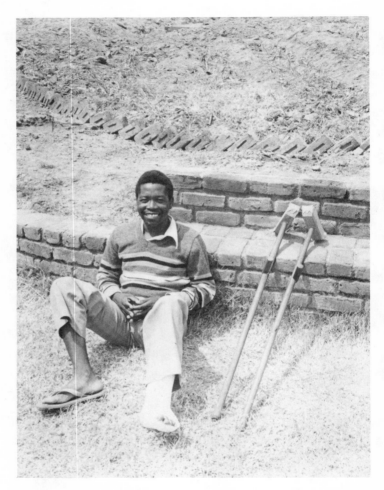

Malawi Bible School student "enjoying" a disabled foot.

16
The Lord Provides

Up at 5:00 a.m. Loaded the car! Cooked thin cornmeal porridge for breakfast. Left at 6:45 a.m. — on schedule.

It was a good trip. Little traffic, and on that one lane of pavement that is always a blessing.

The Nkhotakota road was horrible — mud, ruts, chuckholes. But we made it, 10:00 a.m. on the dot!

First we went to the pastor's house, then on to the church. About twenty people were in attendance. Pastor taught Sunday school from Luke 15. It seemed like a good lesson. At least, there was a lot of discussion.

I preached from John 3:17.

For the noon meal, there was no "relish" [gravy] for the rice and they couldn't buy cooking oil. They didn't know what to do to entertain us properly. I gave them two tins of meat we carried in our car for emergency, and we had a feast!

After lunch the pastor and his wife joined us in a trip on to Nkhotakota town, about twenty miles farther north. I was hoping to find petrol enough to get to my evening destination by the lake. But stations had been closed on Sunday as a rationing measure to save petrol. We were told, "Come back tomorrow!"

While we were there, we decided to see Livingstone's tree where he met a Chechewa chief more than one hundred years ago and presented him a gift of an umbrella. We took pictures of the tree, the pastor and his wife, and an old mosque ruin along the lakeshore. It was a fun afternoon.

We drove the pastor back to his "home" — his four-room hut that he rented for three dollars per month. He had no fields and no support from the local church. I asked him how he found food to feed his family. He answered, "The Lord provides." In addition to what I put in the offering that morning, there was less than five cents. And this man wanted to know how to open a savings account for the church, so he can tithe . . . "The Lord provides."

I left him with a lump in my throat, knowing I was going to a hotel for the night, while his family would have cold rice and leftover tinned meat, by candlelight — but not for atmosphere.

On the way to the hotel we stopped by another church. The evangelist in charge greeted us with tears and called me his brother and his father. He had that very day been praying for me to come. His burning prayer was for a revival in his church.

Because of more rain, the road back was worse than in, I think. We were cautious, especially since our petrol was very low. The Lord assured me He'd taken care of it, but I was hesitant to trust Him.

We arrived without incident at the hotel on the beach where we had fish and chips for supper. We sat and watched the silvery moonbeams dance across the water while the kids played in the sand at the water's edge. A beautiful evening — far removed from a mud hut in Nkhotakota.

I can't forget that pastor.

17

We Clapped Our Hands

Roberts would have pulled out his hair if he had tried to apply his *Rules of Order* in many overseas conferences. Administration of true democracy must be culturally adapted if it is to accomplish its purpose.

Most people who are requested to "chair" annual conferences are steeped in our *Book of Discipline*. That's wonderful — if your conference is in North America. But it doesn't always work the same way in other cultures.

We organize and plan, teach and advise, so our conference will run smoothly and the chairman will not have a nervous breakdown. So far we've been successful. No nervous breakdowns, that is. But there are odd moments. . . .

Like the time the chairman in his stentorian voice called for all delegates to present their credentials. In the stunned silence that followed, the delegates looked at one another and looked at their pastors. The pastors had forgotten. Quickly, scraps of paper, backs of old envelopes, anything to write on was found. Pastors looked around and scribbled down the names of their delegates who were present. Then the delegates proudly presented their "credentials" to the chairman, who was still recovering from shock.

One committee chairman was called upon to report. "No report," was his response. When the chairman of the conference asked whom they wanted for this position for the next year, one venerable old delegate rose to his feet and said, "I think the one we had did a good job. Let's have him for another year." They did, and he did as well the next year.

One year the leader of the conference women was called upon to give her report. She reported all her activities for the year. When she concluded, the chairman asked if there were any questions, and one by one, church leaders rose and testified to the great job she had done. When they were finished, there was a loud burst of applause.

The chairman commented that it was wonderful that they felt happy, and he appreciated their expectations that she would serve another year, but that decision had not been made yet.

This caused considerable confusion among the delegates, who wanted to know what the chairman meant. Realizing that he did not know that at that time the women's leader was chosen by the annual conference, I quietly informed him. He then explained to the conference that even though he had heard their sentiments, the leader had not yet been elected for the coming year.

One older man stood to his feet and said, "What do you mean we haven't elected her? Didn't you hear? We clapped our hands. That means we want her for next year!"

Our chairman said in a pleading voice, "O.K., I understand. You clapped your hands. But please, just for me, if you want her for next year, please raise your hands."

It was unanimous.

18
Big Julius

Big Julius was not particularly good to look at. He had been a troublemaker in bygone days, actually not so far bygone.

I first met Big Julius when stopping for a visit with our pastor in Blantyre. Big Julius was visiting there too. Pastor introduced us. Big Julius was a new Christian. He had been a bad man in trouble with the law, feared by all who knew him.

As I looked at Big Julius, I knew that I'd want him on *my* side. He wasn't one you'd want to fight.

Big Julius had been to South Africa and worked in the mines. He had learned Shangaan there. Wonderful! That was the language I had learned in Zimbabwe. So we could communicate. He didn't know English, and my Chichewa was still in "infancy." We talked and learned about each other. It was an interesting afternoon.

That night we prepared for bed. Pastor had made arrangements for me to stay with a neighbor as his house was full. "Before we go to bed," he said, "it is time for prayers."

The doors opened and in came about forty children from the neighborhood, into a ten-by-twelve room. While the adults were coming in, the children became restless. Big Julius got up. I wondered what he was going to do. He went over to the children and said, "Do you know this song?" and he began to sing,

"Yesu, ndi wa bwino. Yesu, ndi wa bwino. Yesu, ndi wa bwino, ndi wa bwino Kwambiri."

"Again."

"Jesus is so good. Jesus is so good. Jesus is so good, He is so very good."

As I listened and watched, my heart was touched. Big Julius, tough, fearsome, changed and gentle, leading children in singing the goodness of Jesus.

Yes, Jesus is good. His goodness has made a difference in the life of Big Julius and in lives of hundreds like him.

Curious children are responsive to the gospel in Africa . . . and worldwide.

19

Respectfully Yours

Someone once said, "When they passed out 'manners' you thought they said 'bananners,' and you ate yours."

Manners are something to be learned as quickly as possible when working cross-culturally. Good American manners may well be bad African manners. Sometimes we go on being politely impolite for a long time before we learn.

What are good manners? How do you show proper respect in an African setting?

Some things are easy to learn. You never give or receive things with your left hand. *Always* use the right. Practice that. Soon you will be self-conscious if you give or receive something with your left hand.

If someone gives you a gift, you receive it with two hands. Two hands show greater respect for the giver and greater appreciation for the gift. In fact, to give with two hands shows the respect of the giver for the receiver. Often a leader will say, "We receive our visitor with two hands." He means that you, the visitor, are a gift, and he and his people appreciate receiving you.

Another cultural sign of respect in Malawi is the respect a woman shows for her husband. A woman will always kneel or squat when speaking or giving something to her husband. She does likewise when she speaks to anyone for whom she has respect. If you meet her on the path, she may just curtsy to greet you, but if you stop to talk, down she goes. Men sometimes will kneel if they wish to show great respect to the woman to whom they are speaking.

It happened during a women's module. One day the phone rang. A student was calling his wife. I called her to the phone and explained how to hear and speak into the instrument. (Her very first time.) I started to walk away to give her privacy for her call, but looked back to be sure she had it right. She did! I called my wife to come see this supreme example of respect. There the student's wife was, on her knees in my dining room, talking to her husband on the phone. Now, that's good manners!

Another way of showing respect is the way you use the language. Always use plural pronouns when speaking to someone older than yourself, or to someone important, even though he is younger.

When speaking to a man you respect, you should call him "Father" or "Grandfather" (if he is old). The same is true for women, "Mother" or "Grandmother."

One church we visited, the evangelist in charge, nearly twice my age, came to greet us. His English was as severely limited as my Chichewa. As we approached, he came with the greeting, "Daddy! God bless you, Daddy!" I never felt so honored in my entire ministry.

Sometimes we Americans become too informal. It is hard to remember the high office someone has received and refer to him by title, when we have been on a first-name basis for years. In fact, we want to be on a first-name basis with everyone, even strangers. There are some benefits, no doubt. But the warmhearted Malawian can teach us a lot about how to show respect to each other.

20
Out to Dinner

Did I take my wife "out" to dinner! Come with me and I'll show you the place. Close your eyes . . . think . . . imagine . . .

We cross the Zambezi River, wide and deep, at Chirundu. As we drive along the river valley, on our way to Zimbabwe from Malawi, the gnarled, huge, leafless baobab trees stand starkly above the rest of the African bush. The brilliant lilac-breasted roller swoops overhead while the hornbill glides by, close to the car.

"Watch out!" A warthog family is running across the road in front of us, tails held high like little antennae. Herds of gentle impalas are feeding by the roadside, sometimes gracefully leaping into the air as our car surprises them away. A mongoose runs across the road.

"Oops . . ." There's a herd of three young elephants right beside us. As we slam on the brakes to get a better look, they fade back into the bush, disappearing almost instantly. A half mile down the road another elephant — an old bull with long tusks — grazes contentedly, unafraid of us or anything else. A family of waterbuck is in the middle of the road around another curve. They look fluffy, furry, huggable — almost like stuffed toys.

A black and yellow gate looms up in front of us. No worry. It's just the Veterinary Department checking to see if we've picked up any tsetse flies in the valley before we start "up."

Then, up we go, twisting and turning as we climb the steep cliffs of the Zambezi Escarpment. Right at the top is a picnic table and some benches. We stop. Out comes our little gas pot and cooker-top, tablecloth, teapot, cold chicken, "Cup-a-Soup," cheese and crackers, and instant coffee.

We sip our soup and listen to the hippos grunting in the valley below, hear the birds crying from their resting places, watch the sun set across the Zambezi.

As we look at each other and look around us, we know we wouldn't want to be anywhere else.

The gazelle is one of the many beautiful animals of Africa.

21
Seek First

It's about a forty-mile walk from Salima to Damba Village — about one and a half days, if you keep moving.

Damba Church had invited Salima Church to bring a team and hold a weekend revival. They accepted. There was no money for bus fare, so what could they do? Walk!

What would they eat along the way? It was rainy season, so there would be plenty of water to drink.

The pastor brought a small sack of cornmeal made from the maize of his own garden. "If we all bring a sack of meal from our homes and pool our resources of a few cents each, we can perhaps buy some vegetables along the way. We will eat!"

It was agreed. Each brought a small sack of meal, and they put together a treasury of about $1.75. The nine of them then set out early on Friday morning. They followed the pathways. At mealtimes they turned in to the nearest village. They did not know the people, but they asked to borrow a pot to cook their porridge, and they begged a bit of firewood. At every village they were refused. Instead, the people bade them sit and rest while they cooked meal and vegetables for them. They arrived at Damba Village the next afternoon.

The Christian fellowship was wonderful. They held services at two preaching points. Their choir sang in ringing tones. Their feet may have been tired, but their hearts were light. The largest crowd ever gathered at Sambo Turn-off Church heard their message and responded.

Too soon it was time to go home again.

They followed the same pathways but stopped in different places. At mealtimes, they turned again to the nearest villages.

At their last stop, they still had their entire stock of maize-meal and their treasury. They left the meal as a gift for their hosts.

As they set out to do their Master's business, He supplied their every need — just as He said He would!

*   *   *

Malawians are gifted actors, and students enjoy dramatizing Bible events. (See next chapter.)

22
Dramatics

"Eleeya! Eleeya! I have seen King Ah-hab's wickedness. . . ."

Elijah fell to his knees at the sound of the voice of God (coming from the room just off the platform).

If you want to understand a passage of scripture, have Malawians dramatize it. They are gifted actors.

In a recent drama in our church three main events in the life of Elijah were summarized to show how God provides for His people.

You would have laughed at the students, flapping their wings as they ran, flapped, jumped, into the room where God was, and then came with food in their mouths to where Elijah was in prayer. He ate and was sustained.

You would have been moved at the joy of the poor widow and her son as the meal and oil were multiplied after she cooked a bit of cornmeal porridge for the man of God. Our widow was not selfish. She even invited in some of her starving neighbors and cooked a bit of porridge for them as well.

You would have laughed at the prophets of Baal crying a little louder, cutting themselves, all to no avail. And you would have thrilled to see the fire come upon Elijah's sacrifice in response to his prayer of faith. (I think the real Elijah used water, but our students used kerosene and a match and had a real fire in a galvanized bath tub. I was a bit afraid they'd catch their robes afire.)

And when God sent the rain from a cloud the size of a man's hand, the audience clapped in His praise.

It was a service long to be remembered.

That wasn't the only drama I'll remember for a long time. We often do drama for our school chapel services. I will always remember Adam and Eve, wearing fig leaves made from torn pieces of paper bag, hiding from the wrath of God — under a school desk.

I will never forget Mahlon and Chilion, sons of Naomi, sitting with their mother. One said, "Mother, I'm not feeling better." (Klunk!) He fell dead at her feet. Then the other son, "Mother, I'm not feeling better, too." (Klunk, also.)

Later in the story, Boaz looked under his blanket, where he had been snoring blissfully, and saw Ruth sleeping at his feet. "Hm-m-m-m!" he said in a most interested tone of voice. Everyone cracked up. But why not? Boaz was interested, wasn't he?

Drama is a way of studying scripture. Drama is a way of teaching the people in an unforgettable manner. Drama is a way of involving the young people of the church in the service so they become a part of it.

Sometimes you wonder . . . as in the stories of the Prodigal Son and Noah. In both dramas, the students that enjoyed the drama most seemed to be the sinners. Maybe we all can act that part so graphically because it is so close to us.

Abraham offering Isaac on the mountain and Ruth's devotion to Naomi were moving experiences. We were able to visualize in a new way the depth of their commitment. Maybe that is the key to using drama — to help us visualize in a new way God's movement among men.

The Bible is more real to me since I have watched the Malawian dramatically explain what it means to him.

23
District Meeting

The water made shiny streaks down their faces. Cute! But also moving.

It was time for parents to offer their children in dedication to the Lord through baptism. But let me tell you about the whole day.

I arrived at the church at 10:15 a.m. for a 10:30 a.m. service, on a district meeting Sunday. The service actually started at 10:45, with singing of choruses. The call to worship was at 11:15 . . . off to a good start!

After scripture, prayer, and singing, it was time for the baby dedication. Nine sets of parents came forward and stood in a line across the front of the church. Most moms were nursing their babies to keep them quiet.

Questions were asked and answered, then the fathers took their children and knelt. Pastor and his assistant moved from child to child, baptizing them in the name of the Father, Son, and Holy Spirit. The water made little shiny rivulets down their faces and stood in beads on their curly hair. Some cried and some looked in wonder with dark liquid eyes. A special moment.

Choirs sang and adults came for baptism — seventeen of them. Though they were "sprinkled," there was enough water placed on them by the cupped hands of the pastor that some looked as if they'd been "poured," or even "immersed." The cow-dung plastered floor soaked up the droplets that fell. Another special moment.

Choirs sang and adults came to join the church by profession of faith. Twelve people stood proudly,

89

answered the questions, and were received into membership. One child moved from junior membership to adult. Seven adults transferred from other denominations.

Then, there were seven who had been disciplined for drinking or breaking other rules of the church. They had been suspended and were now being reinstated. Since we don't have any procedure for that in our *Book of Discipline,* they were reinstated by the order of the Scottish Presbyterian Church. There was great rejoicing!

What a morning we were having. But the morning was gone and afternoon was well on the way. More choirs, offering, several youngsters reciting memorized scripture, then the sermon.

Dismissal came at 1:30 p.m. But it really wasn't dismissal . . . just recess! It was a welcome break to stretch backs and legs while the pastor and elders prepared for the Lord's Supper. At 2:00 p.m. we reconvened for Communion.

More singing, another sermon. I was getting drowsy, and the babies in the congregation were noticing their lack of lunch. Restless would be an understatement. As their voices mounted higher, so did the pastor's. Out came the "natural pacifiers" and soon most of the little ones were snoozing contentedly in their mothers' arms.

"You who truly and earnestly repent of your sins . . ." The pastor read the invitation and prayers of the Communion service. I was able to follow most of it because I know it in English.

Communion was served differently. There were two stemmed glasses filled with red Kool-Aid (without sugar), and a large tin pot from which the glasses were continually refilled. There was also a basket of broken pieces of bread. We were invited to come, take a piece of bread, kneel, "remember," drink a swallow, then arise and return to our seats. Two blind men were led by the hand to participate. It was a special moment.

Having no organ to play softly, we began to sing. We sang fifteen verses of "Rock of Ages," eight verses of "Power in the Blood," and five verses of "There is a Fountain." It takes a long time to serve 250 people that way, but it was worth it.

Each choir sang its favorite song; then there was a closing prayer. 3:45 p.m. Five hours of celebration.

The Body is alive and well in Malawi!

Everyone happily joins the mealtime food line at church get-togethers, Zimbabwe.

Malawian women cook rice to perfection.

24
Darkest Africa

The yellow flames reflected golden on the circle of black faces around the village fire.

I was a young new missionary on one of my first trips alone into the African bush. We were having a district meeting at an evangelist's village deep in the bush. It was a Saturday night. No moon. I knew almost no Shangaan, and they, no English. The village fire was the only light for miles. I had an idea where the words "darkest Africa" came from.

Though there was darkness around, we felt light and warmth in our little circle. From time to time someone would break the silence with, *"Kurhala!"* (Peace!) Then he or she would give a testimony of God's love and greatness.

After a time of testimonies and choruses, we stood in a circle around the fire, joined hands, and started singing a hymn. I knew the tune and felt wonderfully together with my black brothers and sisters.

Our voices lifted as we thought of the words, I in English, and they in Shangaan. "There is power, power, wonder-working power, in the precious blood of the Lamb. . . ."

Suddenly there was a piercing scream. A young woman just two or three persons to my right was trying to break free of the circle. She threw herself to the ground. Immediately the evangelist and two or three others gripped her and held her down. She was crying out! The "blood of the Lamb" had troubled the evil spirits which were possessing her.

By the flickering firelight I saw the old evangelist

place his hands upon her head. I heard him command, "*Huma! Huma!*" (Come out! Come out!)

While this drama was taking place only a few feet from me, the rest of the people still stood, still held hands, still sang, "There is power, power, power in the blood."

In a few minutes the spirits left the young woman. She was calm. She was *free!* She stood and rejoined the circle. With tears streaming golden down her cheeks, she joined us in singing, "There is power, wonder-working power, in the precious blood of the Lamb!"

*　　*　　*

The people that walked in darkness have
seen a great light: they that dwell in
the land of the shadow of death, upon
them hath the light shined.

— Isaiah 9:2

An African woman, recently freed from satanic powers, expresses her joy.